SOVIET DICTATOR JOSEPH STALIN

CHINESE COMMUNIST CELEBRATION, 1951

Jennifer Fandel

COMMUNISM

CREATIVE EDUCATION

Imagine the most perfect place. There is no crime. No one is poor or hungry. Everyone has a comfortable home and a good job, and all children are excited to

A COMMUNITY IDEA

attend school, which has excellent teachers, small classrooms, and the most up-to-date equipment. In this perfect place, people share what they have and work together toward common goals. While this perfect place does not exist, governments create and enforce laws with this perfect place in mind. Although they realize that there are obstacles—such as time, money, and human nature—that make reaching this level of perfection impossible, most governments strive to improve the lives of their citizens.

The idea of a perfect society is key in the government system known as communism. Communism is based on the idea of a **classless** society, a society that strives to provide equal opportunities to all of its people, especially in terms of income and work. Stemming from the French word *commun*, the word communism refers to group or community ownership of property and industry. This ownership is by the citizens of a nation or by the government on behalf of the citizens. In an ideal communist government, free enterprise and private ownership are nonexistent. Instead, people work together to sustain their community. Each person works as he or she is able. In return, the fruits of their collective labor are equally divided, based upon each person's needs.

Many of the ideas upon which communist governments are based were first laid out in *The Communist Manifesto* of 1848, in which German philosophers Karl Marx (1818–83) and Friedrich Engels (1820–95) presented their vision of a new world involving a classless society that functioned without capitalism. Ideally, they said, a communist system of government would break down the barriers of inequality, eliminating greed and envy, and ultimately making government itself unnecessary, as people would be able to rule themselves.

GERMAN PHILOSOPHER KARL MARX

Yet, rather than a system that leads to the phasing out of government, communism has become a system in which the government has complete control over the people living under it. When Vladimir Lenin (1870–1924) set up the world's first communist country—the Soviet Union—in 1922, he established a **dictatorship** that was meant to remain in power only until the people were strong enough to take over the government. Although Lenin's dictatorial **regime** was to be a transitional phase, it remained in place throughout the Soviet Union's entire history, setting a **precedent** for all communist governments to come. To date, no communist government has gotten past the transitional dictatorship phase, nor has any achieved a state of perfection in which government is unnecessary.

Communist governments usually come to power in times of instability or chaos in a country. It has typically taken force to establish communist governments, as not all citizens easily accept the fundamental **ideology** behind the system, nor have people been willing to give their private businesses and land to the government. In fact, during the past 90 years, most communist governments have come to power through civil war or revolution. In some cases, however, rigged elections in **democratic** countries have put communist governments in power. For example, in the 1948 elections in Czechoslovakia, only communists were placed on the ballots, and election results were falsified, bringing the country under communist power.

Although communist governments were once in place throughout Eastern Europe, the Soviet Union, and many counties in Latin America, Asia, and Africa, only five communist countries remain in the world today: China, Vietnam, Laos, North Korea, and Cuba. Out of the nearly 200 countries in the world, 5 countries may sound insignificant. However, because of the large population of China, nearly one-fourth of the world's people still live under communism. In the 1980s, before the fall of communism in the Soviet Union and Eastern Europe, one-third of the world's population lived under communist regimes.

Soviet Union

STATUE OF VLADIMIR LENIN IN RUSSIA

In 1917, Vladimir Lenin wrote *State and Revolution*, clarifying his ideas about the role of revolution in establishing a communist government. It was published in 1918.

"Democracy is always hemmed in by the narrow limits set by capitalist exploitation, and always remains, in reality, a democracy for the minority, only for the propertied classes, only for the rich.

"Forward development, i.e., toward Communism, proceeds through the dictatorship of the proletariat [laborers]; and cannot do otherwise, for the *resistance* of the capitalist exploiters cannot be *broken* by anyone else or in any other way.

Soviet Union

"The dictatorship of the proletariat imposes a series of restrictions on the freedom of the oppressors, the exploiters, the capitalists. We must suppress them in order to free humanity from wage slavery, their resistance must be crushed by force.

"Only in Communist society, when the resistance of the capitalists has been completely crushed, when the capitalists have disappeared, when there are no classes (i.e. when there is no difference between the members of society as regards their relation to the social means of production), *only* then 'the state . . . ceases to exist,' and it '*becomes possible to speak of freedom*.' Only then will there become possible and be realized a truly complete democracy, a democracy without any exceptions whatever."

RUSSIAN FARMERS UNDER COMMUNISM, 1931

COMMUNIST CUBAN DICTATOR FIDEL CASTRO

All communist countries have similar structures. First and foremost, they allow only one political party: the Communist Party. The Communist Party is the ultimate authority in communist countries. It is the party's job to clarify the laws of the country, the organization of the government, and the structure and goals of the party itself. Most parties make these aims clear through periodic revision of their country's **constitution**.

Within the party, power rests in the hands of the central committee, which is a large group of party policymakers, numbering in the hundreds. The central committee is led by the politburo, a shortened term for "political bureau," numbering around 20 policymakers, who are a step higher in the party. At the very top of the Communist Party is a chairman, known as the secretary general, who guides the party's policymaking. Loyal party members move up in party ranks based on their work leading regional parties, managing government-run enterprises, and supervising government departments. For each move up the party ladder, party members must be nominated by a number of higher-ranked officials.

Despite the party's central role in the policymaking of the country, there are official government positions in addition to the party. Most communist countries have a separate lawmaking body and court system; however, both are controlled by the party. Lawmakers and judges are nominated and voted upon from within the party, so only obedient communists are chosen. Besides making and revising laws for the country, the lawmaking body also selects the head of government. This person, usually known as the president or premier, translates party policies into action. In many cases, the premier and the secretary general of the Communist Party are the same person.

While a president holds the highest position in a communist government, any decisions he makes must be supported by the party. In most situations, presidents serve for life, but they can be deposed if they lead the country or the party in the

Cuba

wrong direction. Such was the case with Nikita Khrushchev (1894–1971), the premier of the Soviet Union from 1957 to 1964. After Khrushchev moved Soviet missiles into Cuba and failed to modernize Soviet agriculture, the party decided to replace him, believing that his troublesome foreign and domestic policies had jeopardized the country's position as one of the world's great powers.

In communist nations, the power of the government is centralized. This means that power is concentrated in the hands of the president and government officials in a capital city, and orders are carried out by regional and local government officials. This is different from other systems of government in which regional or state governments determine many of their own laws and policies.

At the lowest end of the centralized communist government are those party members who work in local or regional government; at the highest are those who lead the national government. At any level, government officials are expected to assign tasks related to the Communist Party's mission to those below them, appoint key staff from within the party's membership, and monitor their performance to uphold party standards. The system is kept in check through two main rules: officials must accept the decisions of those at higher levels, and they may not organize opposition within the party at any level. Those who do not accept these rules are kicked out of the party and their positions.

Communist governments closely manage all aspects of their countries' livelihood—from its arts and sciences to its business and politics. Since the government controls most enterprise, full-time party officials manage and supervise the country's businesses. These businesses usually relate to a country's resources or needs. In China, for example, the government maintains control of the transportation sector, such as the airlines and trains. In the majority of communist countries, because of the importance of a stable food supply, agriculture is managed by the government.

Soviet Union

Because the party in communist countries has complete control of the government and the society as a whole, many citizens view party membership as a way to opportunity since it helps them make connections to those in power. In most communist countries, any time after a citizen turns 18, he or she can register as a party member. Because the Communist Party tries to attract only those who wish to fully support its mission, party officials commonly ask for three recommendations by current members and may place new members on a one-year probation period. Along with paying yearly dues, party members must pledge their total allegiance to the Communist Party.

SOVIET PREMIER NIKITA KHRUSHCHEV

THE COMMUNIST MIND

Communism is a form of government that combines an economic system with a belief system. Citizens are asked to trust in a system that controls their work and divides the products of their labor equally among all citizens. Personal greed should be suppressed. Instead, people should think about how their work improves the lives of all citizens and the country as a whole. Coupled with this economic idea is the belief in an ideal world in which poverty and inequality no longer exist.

When the Communist Party was founded in 1918, its creator, Vladimir Lenin, believed that change would come only through revolution. This belief in revolution hinted at the effects of communist governments on people. Because the people in a communist country need to accept communism wholeheartedly in order for the government to maintain control, political **dissent** is not allowed. In the minds of communist leaders, dissent is unnecessary since the communist way is the "right way." Those who speak out or organize against the government are severely punished with detention or even death. Joseph Stalin (1879–1953), the secretary general of the Soviet Communist Party from 1922 to 1953, was one of the modern world's most ruthless dictators. Responsible for the deaths of millions under Soviet rule, Stalin personally wrote lists of those who were to be punished or even killed because they had spoken out against the government.

Because communist countries have only one political party, and because people are expected to support that party completely, citizens have no right to choose their leader. Popular elections for government officials are largely nonexistent in communist countries, although fraudulent elections—in which the people have no choice but to keep communists in power—are occasionally conducted. In addition, the right to assemble does not exist in most communist countries, and demonstrations are quickly broken up by government officials. In 1956, Hungarians rallied for a

UTOPIAN COMMUNITIES

Communism has its roots in the **socialist** movement of the 1830s. Formed as a result of the poor working conditions and wide class divisions of the Industrial Revolution, the socialist movement promoted phasing out the system that kept ownership of production, distribution, and exchange (such as factories, stores, and banks) in the hands of a few wealthy individuals. Instead, socialists wanted government ownership or cooperative citizen ownership of enterprise. They believed that this would stop the exploitation of the weak, since the socialist system was designed to benefit each person equally. Any surplus income would be distributed in the form of wages for the workers or valuable social services, such as unemployment wages, health insurance, education, and public housing.

Scotland

The word "socialist" was first applied to followers of a British textile factory owner named Robert Owen (1771–1858). In the 1830s, Owen set up a model industrial town in Scotland, in which he provided nonprofit stores, schools, good housing and sanitation, and excellent working conditions for his employees. While most industrialists at the time believed that the exploitation of workers was necessary to produce profit, Owen proved otherwise. His profits at the textile mill grew, and Owen used his findings to promote reforms in factory work.

democratic government in massive street demonstrations in their capital city,
Budapest. Soviet tanks rolled into the crowds, dispersing protestors and killing
more than 3,000.

Additionally, the rights to free speech and freedom of the press do not exist for
citizens within communist countries. Government **censors** closely monitor newspapers, book publishers, and radio and television producers. Communist governments expect that any media produced by their citizens will be praiseful of the government. Claiming that only the truth is being reported, the government's promo-
tion of unbalanced information keeps people unaware of problems or even other
points of view.

Today, however, communist governments may have a harder time keeping people uninformed, as technology now enables people to easily check on life in a neigh-
boring country or learn about new trends on the other side of the globe. Yet, com-

munist countries today try to control even this technology by monitoring the information that enters and leaves the country via e-mail or the Internet. China currently bans more than 19,000 Web sites that government officials consider **subversive** and threatening to the government. Chinese citizens caught sending subversive material over the Internet are often sentenced to two to four years in prison, although they can even be put to death.

Foreign journalists, too, are closely watched, as communist countries want to keep the outside world from learning the full extent of their **human rights** abuses. In many situations, government officials have forced foreign reporters to hand over film, turn over documents, or simply leave the country because their actions have been viewed as controversial. Negative reports about communist countries come mainly from political dissidents who have fled or have found ways to get their stories to journalists or human rights organizations.

Like speech, religious worship is also tightly controlled by communist governments. Most communist governments are wary of religious practice, as it typically requires the assembly of groups and acknowledges that there could be a power higher than the government. Karl Marx referred to religion as the "opiate of the masses." He believed that religion was like opium, a soothing drug, because it made people focus on another world. He felt that if people were focused on spiritual, rather than worldly, matters, they would see no reason to improve things on Earth. In many ways, Marx's ideas have continued in communist governments, which expect their citizens to hold communism above all religions. In fact, while China's constitution grants religious freedom—as long as the religions have registered with the government and are approved—Communist Party officials have stated that citizens who practice their faith openly will not be accepted as members of the party. In North Korea, there is no religious freedom at all. The government monitors religious meetings and sometimes closes down religious meeting places.

Hungary

THE FALL OF THE BERLIN WALL

On November 9, 1989, the East German government decided to open the Berlin Wall, a wall that separated communist East Germany from democratic West Germany. The wall, which was torn down, was both a barrier and a symbol of the divide between the ideas of the **East** and **West**.

Germany

For four decades, from the end of World War II through the 1980s, the United States and the Soviet Union waged a silent war against one another. This war, called the Cold War, was waged over the ideas of communism and democracy. Both countries struggled for supreme power in the world, and they did so through support of other countries. They supplied weapons, military funding, and economic support to struggling countries. Fear was also a strong weapon. By building up their weapons programs, the U.S. and Soviet Union tried to prove their strength.

In the 1980s, under president Ronald Reagan (1911–2004), the U.S. outspent the Soviet Union in the development of weapons. In 1989, the Soviet Union backed down. Soviet premier Mikhail Gorbachev (1931–) declared independence for Soviet-ruled nations, and Poland, Bulgaria, Hungary, Czechoslovakia, Romania, and East Germany all overthrew their communist governments. There was no more need for walls to separate people, governments, and ideas, and the walls came crumbling down.

CELEBRATIONS AT THE FALL OF THE BERLIN WALL, 1989

While restrictions on speech and worship make life difficult for those living under communist governments, perhaps most troubling are the restrictions on movement. Domestic travel is strictly monitored in order to exercise control over citizens. Foreign travel is often prohibited, and professionals who travel for business are carefully watched. Relocation to another country is illegal or, in some cases, made very difficult by the government, requiring endless paperwork and high fees. Those who escape the country illegally are barred from ever returning.

Aside from living with harsh restrictions on their personal rights, citizens of communist countries also often live in poverty, as economic problems plague most communist nations. Shortages of goods are common, resulting from poor government management of enterprise, including delays in material delivery and uneven or slow distribution of goods. Shortages of basic necessities, such as bread, were especially typical in the Soviet Union and Eastern Europe, and, as a result, the government rationed goods. People waited in long lines, sometimes paying for items with wheelbarrows full of devalued money.

Shortages also often result when communist countries collectivize their agriculture. Under collectivization, farmers work for government-owned farms and turn over the products of their labor—their crops and animals—to the government, to be divided among all people in the country. This system, which is much different from farming to feed one's family, is usually quite disturbing to farmers when first implemented. In 1928, when collectivization began in the Soviet Union, farmers slaughtered animals and burned crops to keep their food sources out of government hands. In time, they cut back on their production.

In the history of communism, economic problems have also occurred as governments tried to create classless societies. In trying to view each person as completely equal, communist governments have overlooked the fact that not all people have the same talents and interests. Since the early years of communism, countries

China

CHINESE FARMER HAULING CANOLA PLANTS

have continued to struggle with this idea of equality as they've assigned positions in the workforce. Many governments have fallen back on what is easiest, funneling people into careers based on their parents' career success or their family's ties to the Communist Party. Most countries have found out, however, that progress slides backward if the right people are not in position to keep the economy, culture, and intellectual growth alive.

Another source of economic trouble in communist nations can be found in the wages the government sets, paying people at only a subsistence level. While these wages usually provide the basics for citizens, such as their food, shelter, and clothing, they allow no extra money for people's personal interests. Most capitalist countries believe that a growing economy is dependent upon people wanting and buying what is new, bigger, and better. Communist countries, removed from this mindset, have stagnant economies.

CHINESE STUDENTS CALLING FOR FREEDOMS, 1989

However, as global trade is rapidly expanding, some communist countries have loosened their control on the economy, giving people more opportunity to seek personal gain. Government policies, though, favor those in big cities and have widened the gap between rich and poor. For example, China's entry into the technology and manufacturing sectors has made it one of the fastest growing economies of the world. Yet, in China's countryside, agricultural workers living in small villages have received no extra assistance from the government and are able to grow just enough food to survive.

While people in communist countries usually live in hardship, elite members of the Communist Party enjoy favors such as country homes, vacations, permission to leave the country, and currency to buy foreign goods. Eventually, the economic gap between ordinary citizens and those at the top levels of government grows larger and larger. Critics of communism have called the system government-run capitalism, since those with wealth and power still sit at the top.

VISIONS AND REALITIES

Few people would argue against the ideals that Karl Marx laid out in *The Communist Manifesto*. Communism's original concept—to provide equality and opportunity to people without regard to income or class—was designed to provide numerous benefits to the citizens living under it. According to communist ideals, citizens do not have to worry about providing basic necessities for themselves. The government provides food, shelter, healthcare, and employment, among other basic needs. In addition, citizens receive fair pay for their work, and no one is exploited, overworked, or paid less than what his or her work is worth to the society at large. In such a system, competition is unnecessary, so no one is expected to work harder than anyone else in order to make a business succeed.

China

In the 1950s and '60s, African countries often saw communism as a practical solution to the problems they faced after winning independence from European governments. Since the late 1800s, the majority of countries in Africa had been colonies under the power of such countries as Britain, France, Spain, and Portugal. Once the African nations had their independence, there was a period of chaos and uncertainty within their borders, and many looked for help improving their education systems, developing their natural resources, and raising living standards. Some established alliances with the Soviet Union and Cuba, hoping to get the assistance they badly needed.

Benin

Angola and Benin were two African countries that established communist governments. Benin, on the western coast of Africa, won its independence from France in 1960, becoming a **republic**. Less than five years later, it fell under military rule, and then became a communist country in 1975. Fourteen years later, in 1989, pressure from student and worker protests helped restore the republic. Angola, on the coast of southwest Africa, became a communist country in 1976. In 1990, it transformed its government into a socialist democracy. In this system, there is still government ownership of enterprise, but more than one political party is allowed in the country, and there are open elections.

According to Marx's ideals, communism also doesn't trap workers, as he believed capitalism did, in one specific job and the confines of one economic class for the rest of their lives. Marx didn't believe that only the rich should be able to appreciate art or discuss politics, which is what he saw happening in capitalist systems. In his view, communism would provide complete freedom for citizens to develop themselves into well-rounded individuals. He explained, "Society regulates the general production and thus makes it possible for me to do one thing today and another tomorrow, to hunt in the morning, fish in the afternoon, rear cattle in the evening, criticize after dinner, just as I have a mind, without ever becoming hunter, fisherman, shepherd, or critic."

In many ways, if the system were to function according to Marx's vision, a communist government would be easy to maintain. Production of goods would stay at an even pace, people would do their jobs, and everyone would work toward world harmony. With citizens unified around the common ideals promoted in communism, leaders would not be troubled with the lawlessness that accompanies personal greed and envy.

In an ideal world, the international community would also benefit from communism. In Marx's original conception, communism is a peaceful system that focuses on building community. As countries around the world continue to go to war because of disagreements over property, resources, and ideology, a system that aims to eliminate greed in the world seems like a refreshing change.

Yet, we don't live in an ideal world. In looking at communism's actual successes and failures, many people would argue that the disadvantages of communism far outweigh the advantages. In fact, many of the advantages of communism have never existed in the real world. It has been difficult, if not impossible, to implement the communist vision of the world because it's against human nature to live without want. This has been proven true in many communist governments, most often because of the greed of those in control of the government.

Unemployment, rationing, poverty, and even malnutrition have been some of the effects of communism. Communist governments and government-run enterprises are poorly managed, and citizens suffer the consequences. While citizens are usually paid subsistence wages, there have also been times in communist governments when financial problems meant that citizens went without pay. In the 1980s, for example, government mismanagement of Soviet and Eastern European enterprises led to meager, if not nonexistent, wages at a time when the countries were experiencing huge price increases. A common saying at the time in Poland was, "We pretend to work and they pretend to pay us."

The lack of choice is also difficult for many citizens living under communist governments, who are forced to follow the party, accept whatever job is given them, and not desire any more than they have. In such a system, people feel little incentive to work. Government-controlled enterprises keep people working at an even pace, whether faced with a lot of work or very little, so even a simple choice—to work hard—is taken from citizens. Additionally, while government managers understand how their workers help sustain the communist system, workers themselves may feel like puppets within the system. They have no ability to act on their own.

For citizens who have lived unhappily under communism, its worst aspect is the feeling of helplessness under the repressive government. Vaclav Havel (1936–), a Czech writer who served as the president of the Czech Republic as it emerged from communism in 1989, tried to express this frustration and explain the mindset of those who live under communism. He wrote, "They need not accept the lie. It is enough for them to have accepted their life with it and in it. For by this very fact, individuals confirm the system, fulfill the system, *are* the system." While citizens are forced to live with the government, some manage to **defect** from their countries

Poland

and obtain political asylum, which allows them to become citizens of a new country. Such was the case for Russian ballet dancer Rudolf Nureyev (1938–93) who, when on tour in France in 1961, refused to board a plane back to the Soviet Union. The Soviet government had tightly controlled his career, and he believed that more opportunity would come to him if he left his country.

While the citizens living under a communist government suffer the most, even government officials are often vulnerable to the repression built into the system. In 1956, after Joseph Stalin's death, his successor, Nikita Khrushchev, made a secret speech in which he criticized Stalin's repressive government, known for its terror

CZECH WRITER AND PRESIDENT VACLAV HAVEL

campaigns and killings. In the middle of the speech, one Communist Party member
yelled out, "And where were you, Comrade Nikita Sergeyevich, when these crimes
were occurring?" Upon hearing this, Khrushchev demanded that the person who
spoke out stand and identify himself. Silence fell over the room, and no one stood.
Khrushchev then said, "I was then, comrade, where you are now."

While communist leaders expect their people to work for the common good,
setting aside their own greed, government officials themselves often fail to do this.
Many officials use their positions of power to gain more power and wealth while
leaving their country's workers without the necessities they were promised in return
for their labor. Because political dissent is forbidden, government officials believe
they won't be reported and punished for corruption and organized crime, such as
involvement in gambling, prostitution rings, and drug smuggling. Even when corruption is exposed, it is difficult to punish because it is usually widespread, even

ONE OF ONE MILLION NORTH KOREAN SOLDIERS

among high-ranking government officials and those in law enforcement.

Because corruption tends to run rampant in communist governments, the international community struggles to deal with communist countries. The high occurrence of human rights abuses in these nations creates large numbers of refugees, and the world at large must find a home for these political dissidents. Also, the world puts its resources toward maintaining the health and safety of citizens living under communist governments by providing international aid in some communist countries. In North Korea, for example, international aid organizations, including the United Nations World Food Program, feed almost all children under the age of seven. Without this aid, the children would suffer the devastating effects of malnutrition.

The international community must also deal with communist leaders' never-ending quest for power, which can threaten the security of other nations. In 1962, for example, Cuban prime minister Fidel Castro (1926–) allowed installations for Soviet nuclear missiles to be positioned in his country. Castro wanted the U.S. to recognize Cuba's power, and the tense standoff that followed threatened to erupt into a full-scale nuclear war. Today, world leaders and foreign policy experts watch communist dictators closely, making sure that they don't disrupt the stability and peace of the world.

Likewise, world leaders are also concerned about how communist nations will survive in the present global marketplace, as impoverished and repressive nations tend to breed both local and international conflict. If a communist country feels isolated from the rest of the world, it may turn to desperate measures in order to gain a position of power. For example, while North Korea is extremely poor, it has the fourth-largest military in the world and funnels much of its money into the development of weapons, including nuclear weapons. Many international leaders encourage communist countries to loosen their controls on enterprise, hoping that greater

North Korea

PRAGUE SPRING, 1968 (TOP); VELVET REVOLUTION, 1989 (BOTTOM)

THE PRAGUE SPRING AND THE VELVET REVOLUTION

The Eastern European country of Czechoslovakia was the breeding ground for two important anti-communist revolutions. The first revolution, which took place in 1968, has been called the Prague Spring for the "thawing" of communist rules and the hope it gave the Czech people. President Alexander Dubcek (1921–92) believed that the communist government was too repressive and promised citizens that he would deliver "socialism with a human face." Restrictions on the economy were loosened, and the Communist Party lessened its control of culture and censorship. Czech citizens fully supported the change, but the Soviet Union didn't. Soviet troops invaded the country, ending Dubcek's presidency and kicking out many leaders of the Communist Party who were sympathetic to Dubcek's aims.

Czech Republic

Twenty-one years later, Czechoslovakia was the scene of the Velvet Revolution, a smooth transition from communism to democracy. Due to the pressure felt during massive antigovernment demonstrations, communist leaders resigned in November 1989. The following month, a democratic government was established. Czech writer Vaclav Havel was elected president, and over the next three years, Czechoslovakia transitioned to a capitalist economy, bid farewell to the Soviet troops occupying the country, and held its first **parliamentary** elections.

economic stability will lead to more stable countries, and the exposure to new ideas will help them establish better relations with the rest of the world.

The idea behind the communist government system stems back to ancient Greece (800–100 B.C.). In writings from that time, philosophers talked of a "golden age" when people didn't own property and lived in harmony together on the land. Many historians believe, however, that even the ancient Greeks may have been passing along legends of the way people dreamed the world might someday be. In the 16th century, these ideas were furthered with the book *Utopia* by English writer Sir Thomas More (1478–1535). In his book, More described a perfect world, or utopia, in which people share ownership of property. He believed that individual ownership encouraged selfishness and created communities that didn't work together.

Throughout history, people consistently turned to these ideas of communal living, many times out of necessity. For example, many Native American tribes before the arrival of Christopher Columbus (1451–1506) in 1492 lived in communities in which they divided the workload and shared the fruits of their labor. In their view, the world was created to be shared. Throughout history, various religions and cultures have adopted this view.

In Europe, however, inequalities influenced people's desire for communal ownership. From the 6th through 19th centuries, property was owned privately by powerful, wealthy landlords, with the poorest people in society being dependent on that land. They worked the land as farmers and had to pay a tax—either in money or goods produced—to the landlord. Because of this situation, the poor were against land ownership, as they could never imagine having land or power of their own.

In the late 19th century, the modern form of communism developed, with the

first true communist government being established in the Soviet Union. In the October Revolution of 1917, Russian Vladimir Lenin and the Bolsheviks, his revolutionary followers, overthrew the temporary government established after the Russian **monarchy** fell. A year later, they established the Communist Party.

After Lenin took control of the government, a civil war erupted between the Bolsheviks and the Mensheviks, who disagreed with Lenin's vision of a government run by the proletariat, or laborers and peasants. Lenin's followers eventually won, setting up a new country called the Union of Soviet Socialist Republics (USSR) in 1922. While this was a huge step for communism, it was Joseph Stalin's version of communism that would shape the future of the country, communism, and the whole world.

As Soviet dictator from 1929 to 1953, Stalin rewrote the aims of communism. He defined it as an **authoritarian** government organized around specific communist ideals. He helped install communist governments throughout Eastern Europe and established ties with the developing communist government in China. Stalin wanted to spread Soviet influence around the globe and hoped to make the country one of the world's major powers.

In order to strengthen the Soviet Union, Stalin started the country on a strict plan toward mass industrialization and collectivized agriculture, placing almost everything under government control. Seeing how rapidly Stalin transformed Soviet society both amazed and scared the rest of the world. What the world didn't see, however, was the brutal dictatorship of terror and intimidation that Stalin established in order to bring about this transformation. Under Stalin's regime, secret police killed more than one million intellectuals and dissidents. Even more were sent to labor camps in Siberia, where the inhumane conditions brought sickness or death. People's lives were harshly controlled, but from the outside, the country appeared unified, strong, and productive. Because of the apparent success of the Soviet Union under Stalin, the Communist Party believed that communism would take root around the world in only 30 years after Stalin's death in 1953.

After Stalin's death, however, the new premier, Nikita Khrushchev, admitted that communism appeared powerful because it brutally repressed its citizens. The Soviet Union then underwent a period called "de-Stalinization" to reform the government. Because of continued corruption in the Communist Party, the government fell into many periods of difficulty over the next four decades. Finally, on December 31, 1991, the Soviet Union dissolved. Countries under Soviet influence, as well as former Soviet republics, were given the freedom to choose their own governments.

The Chinese Communist Party grew up alongside the Communist Party in the Soviet Union. Founded in 1921, it struggled for its first 25 years to get widespread support, while the Chinese government unsuccessfully made its transformation to a republic after thousands of years as a monarchy. In 1935, a Chinese communist

Soviet Union

Soviet tank factory, c. 1940s

NORTH KOREAN DICTATOR KIM JONG IL

SELLING COMMUNISM, BELIEVING COMMUNISM

Throughout history, communist countries have often relied on the use of propaganda to recruit citizens to the Communist Party and encourage their loyalty. In China, colorful posters portrayed communist leader Mao Zedong (1893–1976) as the wise teacher or elder statesman. Mao also published the *Little Red Book of Quotations* in 1966, which provided citizens with ideas of which he approved.

North Korea

In North Korea, propaganda has helped fuel fear in the country. Currently, all families in North Korea must display images of their previous leader Kim Il Sung (1912–94) and their present leader Kim Jong Il (1942–) in their homes. They must make sure that the pictures are clean at all times. Displaying dusty or dirty pictures is considered an act of dissent.

Youth leagues are one of the most popular ways to spread propaganda and encourage party participation from a very young age. In the Soviet Union, the Komsomal youth league automatically entered children into the Soviet Communist Party at a specific age. In Vietnam today, the Ho Chi Minh Community Youth League introduces children to communist ideas in the hope that they will know no others. Taking away choices makes it appear that communism is the only way.

CHINESE DICTATOR MAO ZEDONG WITH SCHOOLCHILDREN

named Mao Zedong and his supporters began "The Long March," a trip of 6,215 miles (10,000 km) on foot from central to northwest China. While the original purpose of the march was to escape attacks from the government's army, which viewed Mao as a threat to the republic, the march ended up inspiring thousands of Chinese citizens, especially peasant farmers, to join the Chinese Communist Party. In 1949, under Mao, the communist People's Republic of China was established. By 1950, the Chinese communists controlled all of China except Taiwan, giving them power over the most populous nation in the world.

In 1958, Mao instituted a policy that he called the Great Leap Forward. The policy, which included a government takeover of all industrial production and collectivization of business and agriculture, failed badly. Peasants didn't meet agricultural quotas, and poor harvests led to one of China's worst famines. Mao blamed the sparrows for the problems and ordered the citizens to kill them. This left the remaining crops to be eaten by insects. Between 1959 and 1962, around 20 million Chinese people died.

In 1966, Mao tried to overhaul Chinese society again. This time, he introduced the Great Proletariat Cultural Revolution. As part of this program, he forced intellectuals and workers to trade places. Believing that an end to formal education would stop an elite class from forming, Mao closed schools and required children to work in the fields. The country fell into shambles, yet the Cultural Revolution didn't end until 1976 with Mao's death.

In 1981, Deng Xiaoping (1904–97) took power and opened China to foreign, capitalist ideas. He encouraged students to attend universities abroad, hoping they would bring new ideas back to rebuild China. He didn't expect the students to be influenced by the democratic governments they learned about while away. In 1989, students staged a pro-democracy rally in Beijing's Tiananmen Square. The rally was squelched, and many students were killed. This opened the world's eyes to China's

China

human rights policies, many of which remain unchanged up to the present time.

While human rights abuses may be common in China, they are out of control in North Korea. After World War II, the Soviet Union occupied the northern half of Korea, while the U.S. occupied the south. The Koreans in the North then adopted their own communist government, united under the Korean Workers' Party. North Korea's formal name is the Democratic People's Republic of Korea, but the name doesn't accurately describe the situation in the country. While the government has a legislature, or lawmaking body, and system of justice, all is under the control of the Korean Workers' Party.

The Korean government carries out severe punishments for all crimes involving disobedience to the government. A mandatory death penalty is given to those who defect from the country or attempt to defect, those who **slander** the government, and those who listen to foreign broadcasts, write letters against the government, or possess antigovernment books. Some executions have been carried out publicly as a warning to workers, university students, and schoolchildren. Additionally, the country has 150,000 to 200,000 people detained for political reasons, many of them in high-security camps in remote areas of the country. Because of the conditions in the camps, the detainees don't always make it out alive.

While many countries believe the remaining communist governments are too repressive to survive, people throughout the world still look to Marx's ideas, dreaming of a government that brings equality and opportunity to the poor and downtrodden in the world. For many, this vision of a transformed world—without greed and war—is idealistic, yet still worth working toward. But, for all of communism's high ideals, governments who use this system must do a better job of mixing dreams with reality. Communism will only live on if governments under this system make a commitment to creating a better world for their people.

China

PROTEST BANNER IN TIANANMEN SQUARE, 1989

1848

Karl Marx and Friedrich Engels publish *The Communist Manifesto*.

1917

Vladimir Lenin and the Bolsheviks succeed at overthrowing Russia's temporary government.

1918

Lenin establishes the Communist Party.

1921

The Chinese Communist Party organizes in Shanghai, China.

1922

The world's first communist country, the Soviet Union, is established.

1945

Korea's north comes under Soviet control; in 1947, the North Koreans establish their own communist government.

1946

The first Eastern European communist government is set up in Albania.

1949

Mao Zedong formally establishes the People's Republic of China and soon enters an alliance with the Soviet Union.

1959

Cuban prime minister Fidel Castro sets up a communist government.

1960

The Chinese Communist Party and Soviet Communist Party end their 10-year alliance.

1968

Czechoslovakia attempts to loosen communist rule. In response, the Soviet Union tightens its control over all Eastern European countries.

Chile

1970

Salvador Allende becomes president of Chile; his government includes
a coalition of socialist and communist supporters.

1975

The African country of Benin becomes a communist country.

Vietnam

1976

Vietnam's north and south are unified under communist rule.

1976

The Soviet Union and Cuba help support a communist government in the southern African
nation of Angola.

1989

Mikhail Gorbachev grants independence to countries under Soviet influence. By the next year,
all communist governments in central and Eastern Europe have collapsed.

1989

China's pro-democracy movement is crushed in Beijing's Tiananmen Square.

1991

The Soviet Union dissolves, and its 15 republics become independent nations.

1992

Vietnam's constitution names the Communist Party as the country's only party;
the country also loosens regulations on the economy.

1993

China's Communist Party announces that free enterprise will be encouraged in the country.

GERMANS PEERING THROUGH THE BERLIN WALL, 1966

authoritarian A type of government that requires strict obedience to authority, such as the president, military, and police. Disobedience is harshly punished.

capitalism An economic system built on individual investment in enterprise and private ownership. Those who use the system are called capitalists.

censors People who review and ban or remove controversial parts of books, newspapers, or television broadcasts.

classless Without economic class distinctions, such as lower, middle, and upper class. In many cases, such class distinctions also determine people's social status.

constitution The basic ideas by which a country is governed, particularly as they relate to the powers of government and the rights of citizens.

defect To leave one's country and become the citizen of another. People defect for political reasons or to escape harsh treatment from their government.

democratic A term used to describe governments based on citizen participation. In most democracies, citizens vote for officials to represent their interests.

dictatorship A government ruled by one person with absolute power (a dictator), usually a tyrant who abuses his or her power and oppresses people.

dissent Disagreement with accepted policies, especially regarding governments. Those who disagree are called dissidents.

East A term used to describe the countries of Asia and the communist nations of Eastern Europe. People often use the term to exaggerate differences between the East and governments and cultures in the West.

economic Relating to the production and distribution of wealth. Countries with strong economies often have wealthier citizens than those with weak economies.

free enterprise Private ownership and management of businesses without government control. Capitalist countries believe in free enterprise.

human rights Rights believed to belong universally to every person, such as the right to live and to speak freely without fear of detention or torture from a government.

ideology A specific belief or idea, such as communism, that serves as the foundation for specific actions or ways of thinking.

Germany

monarchy A government in which the power is held by one person who rules for life, and who has inherited the position from his or her parent.

parliamentary Having to do with the parliament, a group of officials elected to make laws in a country. Many countries in Europe have a parliament.

precedent A previous case or example that influences future action. One can only determine a precedent in hindsight, once similar actions have taken place.

propaganda Organized publicity in the form of posters, pictures, books, and television broadcasts to arouse feelings in people, such as admiration for or fear of a political figure.

regime Specific system of government under one person. Each dictator sets up his own regime according to his personality and style of government.

republic A form of government in which government officials represent citizens. Republics are often, but not always, democratic.

slander To portray or speak negatively of people in a way that harms their reputation or makes them feel threatened.

socialist Relating to a system of government based on government-run enterprise. Communism goes one step beyond socialism, as its goal is to progress to public ownership of enterprise and all aspects of government.

subversive Against or undermining the government. Communist governments have the ultimate say in what they believe is subversive.

West A term used to describe the developed nations in Western Europe and North America. The term often implies countries with democratic governments.

BIBLIOGRAPHY

Central Intelligence Agency. *The World Factbook 2006.*
   http://www.cia.gov/cia/publications/factbook

Fernandez-Armesto, Felipe. *Ideas that Changed the World.* New York: Dorling Kindersley, 2003.

Krieger, Joel, ed. *The Oxford Companion to Politics of the World.* New York: Oxford University Press, 1993.

Lewis, James R., and Carl Skutsch, eds. *The Human Rights Encyclopedia.* Armonk, New York: Sharpe Reference, 2001.

Pious, Richard M. *Governments of the World.* 3 Vols. New York: Oxford University Press, 1998.

agriculture 12, 20, 23, 34, 39
   collectivization 20, 34, 39

Albania 42

Allende, Salvador 43

Angola 24, 43

Benin 24, 43

Berlin Wall 18

Bolsheviks 33, 42

Britain 15, 24, 32

Bulgaria 18

capitalism 4, 8, 22, 23, 25, 31, 32,
   39

Castro, Fidel 29, 42

censorship 16, 31

Chile 43

China 6, 12, 17, 23, 34, 37, 39, 40,
   42, 43

classes 4, 8, 15, 20, 23, 25, 39

Cold War 18

Communist Party 11, 12, 13, 14, 17,
   22, 23, 26, 28, 31, 33, 34, 37,
   39, 42, 43

constitution 11, 17, 43

corruption 28–29, 34

Cuba 6, 12, 24, 29, 42, 43

Czech Republic 26

Czechoslovakia 6, 18, 31, 42

defection 26–27, 40

democracy 6, 8, 16, 18, 24, 31, 39,
   40, 43

demonstrations 14, 16, 31

Deng Xiaoping 39

de-Stalinization 34

detention 14, 34, 40

dictatorship 6, 8, 14, 29, 33, 34

dissent 14, 17, 28, 29, 34, 37

Dubcek, Alexander 31

East Germany 18

economy 14, 18, 20, 22, 23, 25, 31,
   32, 43

elections 6, 14, 24, 31

Engels, Friedrich 4, 42

enterprise 4, 6, 11, 12, 15, 20, 22,
   23, 24, 26, 29, 39

executions 14, 17, 34, 40

France 24, 27

free enterprise 4, 43

free speech 16, 17, 20

Gorbachev, Mikhail 18, 43

Great Leap Forward 39

Great Proletariat Cultural
   Revolution 39

Greece 32

Havel, Vaclav 26, 31

human rights 17, 29, 40

Hungary 14, 16, 18

Industrial Revolution 15

industrialization 34

Internet 17

jobs 4, 25, 26

justice system 11, 40

Khrushchev, Nikita 12, 27–28, 34

Kim Il Sung 37

Kim Jong Il 37

Laos 6

legislature 11, 40

Lenin, Vladimir 6, 8, 14, 33, 42
   State and Revolution 8

Mao Zedong 37, 39, 42
   Little Red Book of Quotations 37
   The Long March 39

Marx, Karl 4, 17, 23, 25, 40, 42
   The Communist Manifesto 4,
   23, 42

media 16, 17, 40

Mensheviks 33

military 18, 24, 29

More, Sir Thomas 32
   Utopia 32

Native Americans 32

North Korea 6, 17, 29, 37, 40, 42

Nureyev, Rudolf 27

October Revolution 33

Owen, Robert 15

Poland 18, 26

Portugal 24

Prague Spring 31

proletariat 8, 33, 39

propaganda 37

property 4, 6, 25, 32

Reagan, Ronald 18

religion 17, 20, 32

republic 24, 34, 39, 40, 43

revolution 6, 8, 14, 15, 31, 33, 39

Romania 18

Russia 27, 33, 42

Scotland 15

shortages 20

socialism 15, 24, 31, 43

Soviet Union 6, 12, 14, 16, 18, 20,
   24, 26, 27–28, 29, 31, 33, 34,
   37, 40, 42, 43

Spain 24

Stalin, Joseph 14, 27–28, 33–34

Taiwan 39

Tiananmen Square 39, 43

travel 20, 23

United Nations World Food Program
   29

United States 18, 29, 40

Velvet Revolution 31

Vietnam 6, 37, 43

West Germany 18

World War II 18, 40

Published by Creative Education

P.O. Box 227, Mankato, Minnesota 56002

Creative Education is an imprint of The Creative Company.

Design by Rita Marshall

Printed in the United States of America

Photographs by Alamy Images (James Frank, Roger Hutchings, Lebrecht
Music and Arts Photo Library, Mary Evans Picture Library, Iain Masterson,
Visual Arts Library), Corbis (The Art Archive, Bettmann, REINHARD
KRAUSE / Reuters, Jacques Langevin, Peter Turnley), Getty Images (AFP,
Express / Stringer, Hulton Archive, MPI / Stringer, Time Life Pictures)

Illustration copyright © 2006 Etienne Delessert (36)

North Korea

Library of Congress Cataloging-in-Publication Data

Fandel, Jennifer.

Communism / by Jennifer Fandel.

p. cm. — (Forms of government)

Includes index.

ISBN-13: 978-1-58341-531-3

1. Communism. 2. Communist state. I. Title.

JC474.F36 2007   321.9'2–dc22   2006020150

First edition

2 4 6 8 9 7 5 3 1